How to Relaunch Your Book: Use this Step-by-Step Proven Program to Bring Your Book Back to Life

(The Work from Home Series: Book 7)

By

Sam Kerns

Books by Sam Kerns

How to Work from Home and Make Money: 10 Proven Home-Based Businesses You can Start Today (Work from Home Series: Book 1)

How to Build a Writing Empire in 30 Days or Less (Work from Home Series: Book 2)

How to Start a Home-Based Food Business: Turn Your Foodie Dreams into Serious Income (Work from Home Series: Book 3)

How to Brand Your Home-Based Business: Why Business Branding is Crucial for Even the Smallest Startups (Work from Home Series: Book 4)

How to Publish a Book on Amazon: Real Advice from Someone Who's Doing it Well (Work from Home Series: Book 5)

The Writer's Toolbox Boxed Set

The Weekend Writer: How to Write a Non-Fiction Book in 2 Months, Even if You Have a Full-Time Job (Work from Home: Book 6)

How to ReLaunch Your Book: Use This Step-by-Step Proven Program to Bring Your Book Back to Life (Work from Home: Book 7)

Sign up at RainMakerPress.com to receive advanced notice of new books in the series!

Table of Contents

Introduction: Can You Really Bring a Stagnant Book Back to Life?

When I first began publishing books on Amazon, I had no idea how things really worked. I believed that if I published a good book, it would bring in passive income for years to come. My plan then was to publish books every few months and build a backlist that automatically produced income every month. And so when I published my first two books and they became bestsellers, I thought I was golden—all I had to do was sit back and collect the income from them every month.

So imagine my surprise when the sales began tapering off.

I couldn't understand what was happening—why were the books that had been so popular just a few short months ago suddenly sinking in the rankings? I desperately tried to revive them by running an occasional promotion, and while they would rise in the ranks temporarily, they would ultimately sink again.

And that got me thinking. What if there was a way to keep the books in my backlist selling consistently so I could increase my sales every month? What if I didn't have to push myself to write a book a month to keep the sales coming in, but could also rely heavily on my backlist for passive sales? I'd heard people talk about this but when I tried their methods, I didn't see the results I wanted. So, I decided to look for a formula that would work for me—and I found it. Once I realized how simple it was, I decided to make it the subject of my next book—and that's what you're reading now.

Here's the truth: There are millions of books on Amazon and your book is only one of them. We all see the bestsellers and those in the top 1,000, but what about all the other books? After all, how can a book sell if no one ever sees it?

Some of the reasons a book doesn't sell are obvious—I can immediately see the problem just by looking at some product pages. But others are more difficult to figure out. In this book, I'll address both the books that saw some success but then experienced a fall in sales, as well as the books that never achieved any sales other than friends and family. Trust me, if you've gone to the trouble to write a book, it's possible to revive it and see some sales.

Here are a few figures to help you wrap your mind around the possibilities:

- According to Author Earnings 2017 report, 487,298,000 eBooks are sold each year on Amazon.
- Those eBooks total more than $1,756,000 a day in sales.
- eBooks aren't the only books selling, in fact they only account for 42 percent of sales. Amazon also sells 675,000,000 printed books a year.

What's keeping you from getting a piece of that pie? That's what we're going to explore in this book. I hope that after reading it, you'll realize your books aren't destined to only sell for a short period of time and then sink into oblivion. That simply doesn't have to be the case.

But I wanted to do more than *tell* you how to perform the necessary steps to revive your book, so I decided to use my first book, *How to Work from Home and Make Money* as an example so I could *show* you how it's done. Before I began writing this book, I let *How to Work from Home and Make Money* fall in the ranks to the sad ranking of 200,853, but after my relaunch, it had the bestseller tag proudly displayed next to it in 2 categories. (See screenshots below)

How did that happen? I used the exact same step-by-step process I'm going to tell you about in this book. And once your book has climbed the ranks, you'll need to use my process to keep it there—otherwise it will just quickly sink again and you'll be back where you started from.

Remember, your book can't sell unless it's seen by the millions of people who visit Amazon every month. Your first job is to first make sure you're presenting the best book you can, and then get it in front Amazon's visitors.

But before we get into the nitty gritty of relaunching a book, or bringing a stagnant book back to life, let's talk about some facts and figures that I think will help you understand the process. Here are 6 things you should know about publishing a book on Amazon according to the 2017 Author Earnings Report.

- Despite the fact that the major publishers and even book sellers like Barnes & Noble, Target, and Walmart saw a decrease in printed book sales, Amazon saw a

15% increase in them last year. If your book isn't available in print, it's time to change that now.

- Even though the top 5 publishers lamented the fact that their eBook sales were falling, Amazon saw a 4 percent increase in eBook sales last year.
- Amazon sells one-half of all print books from the big publishers.
- Kindle Unlimited accounts for 14 percent of all eBooks that are read by Amazon customers. If your book isn't enrolled in KDP Select, you should seriously consider it. In fact, you won't be able to complete all the steps I outline in this book unless it is.
- Audible, which is owned by Amazon, says its customers listened to about 2 billion—that's with a "B"—hours of audiobooks last year. In 2014, that number was only 1 billion. You're missing out on a lot of sales if your book isn't available as an audio book.
- Amazon has 80 million Prime members, which are mostly composed of affluent Americans. That's a built-in marketplace like no other. Later, I'll talk about how I believe my book relaunch helped me score an invitation to be a part of the program and a bonus check from Amazon.

In other words, if you're going to sell books, Amazon is the place to do it. With that big of a pie, there is no reason why you shouldn't be selling books—a lot of them. And that's true even if your book is old or has sunk to the bottom of the rankings.

I need to say something here. I'm not promising that a poorly written book will sell well on Amazon. The plan that I'll lay out in the next few chapters is designed to work for quality books that have been tweaked to perfection. There is a lot of hype that says any book can sell on Amazon, but if you look at all the books that rank in the millions, you'll quickly realize that it's just not true. In order for your book to sell, you must be committed to making it the best it can be. But don't worry, we'll cover exactly how to do that in upcoming chapters.

Are you pumped? Can you see how the possibilities are endless? The truth is, Amazon is a huge marketplace with millions of buyers who have their fingers hovering over the buy button. And if you want to bring your book back to life so they'll buy it, you'll need to take some specific steps.

Let's take a look at my step-by-step plan now and see if we can't get your book selling.

Chapter One: How to Analyze Your Book to Pinpoint its Weaknesses

Every book can be improved, no matter how well it sells. Don't believe me? Just take a look at some of Amazon's bestselling books and scroll down to read the reviews. Among all those 4 and 5 star reviews, you'll inevitably see some 1 and 2 star reviews. That's because whatever the reviewer was looking for in that particular book wasn't there. And that can be true even if a hundred other people thought it was the best book they ever read.

For example, my bestselling book, _How to Build a Writing Empire in 30 Days or Less_ has some shining reviews and I've heard from many readers how it has changed their work lives, but it also has some less than favorable ones. The book is good and was written from years of experience as a freelance writer, but some reviewers didn't seem to understand the premise of the book. That's okay, the method outlined in the book isn't for everyone—only those who are willing to work hard to build a profitable freelance writing business. But a lot of people do get it and the book sells like crazy.

In order for you to relaunch your book to success, you'll need to conduct a deep analysis of your book's strengths, weaknesses and missing pieces. Now, I'm not talking about simply making sure the book is as good as it can be, although that's important too. I'm talking about taking your book apart and putting it back together to make it the best it can be.

Ready? Let's talk about how you'll need to look at your book with a critical eye to determine how to make it sales worthy.

Start with the Cover

You hear a lot about the importance of covers, and there a good reason for that. If a book's cover isn't great, it's not going to sell—period. But where I differ from a lot of other people is that I don't believe you have to spend a fortune to get a good cover. In fact, my two bestselling book covers were created by me for free on Canva.com in about an hour.

But a great book cover needs to have some common traits, and luckily, the right ones are easy to identify. Here are the things your book's cover must have in order to sell.

- **It must match your genre.** One of the biggest mistakes newbie writers make is creating a cover that is so far out of line with what people who love the genre are used to, the buyers don't recognize it as a book they would enjoy. For example, if you write sweet romance books, don't create a cover with a mysterious feel or dark edge to it or your readers will pass it by. The same is true for nonfiction. If you write books about how to use technology to better your business, don't put a cute animal or curvy print on your cover. While this may seem like simplistic advice, I urge you to check out some of the books that are published on Amazon and see just how many inappropriate covers you find. Luckily, the solution is easy. In order to determine whether or not your cover is hindering your sales, take a look at the bestselling books in your genre and model your new cover after those. Remember, you don't want to copy other books, but you should make note of the colors they use, the fonts, and style. Readers of your genre expect to see certain things on the covers of the books they read, and although it's tempting to design yours "outside the box," it won't help your sales. Instead design your cover with the key aspects of bestselling books in your genre.
- **You don't have to spend a lot of money.** Even if you don't have an eye to design your own book cover, you won't need to spend a lot of money to create a cover that sells. Instead, use my guy Nathanial Dasco at nathanieldasco@gmail.com, (He only charges $30 for awesome cover designs) or use his cool new tool at ecoverdesignpro.com. For only $17, you can design your own covers for your eBooks, print, and audio books.
- **Don't only rely on your opinion.** When people look for books on Amazon, they first see thumbnails of the book covers, and they make their decision in a split second about whether or not to click on that book. That's how important your book cover is, so it makes sense to get a few opinions before you decide on one. Instead of asking friends and family, you should reach out to people who read books in your genre and give them a few choices to choose from. (Remember, you can have a book cover professionally designed for only $30, so it

won't cost a fortune to ask for a couple of choices.) Next, you can conduct a survey on social media asking people to vote on a cover using free sites like SurveyMonkey.com or https://www.google.com/forms. If you don't have a big or active social media following, you can conduct an online focus group on sites like PickFu.com for only $20 where people who read your type of books will give you feedback on your cover designs.

The key to selecting a cover that sells is taking yourself out of the equation. It's easy to get so wrapped up in your own preferences when it comes to your book cover that you can easily sabotage your sales. For example, I first designed my own cover for *How to Publish a Book on Amazon*, and was shocked when this highly rated book didn't meet my sales expectations. So I had Nathan design a new cover for it, and it immediately began to take off. Personally, I prefer my cover, but the buyers on Amazon obviously prefer Nathan's. Here's the before and after.

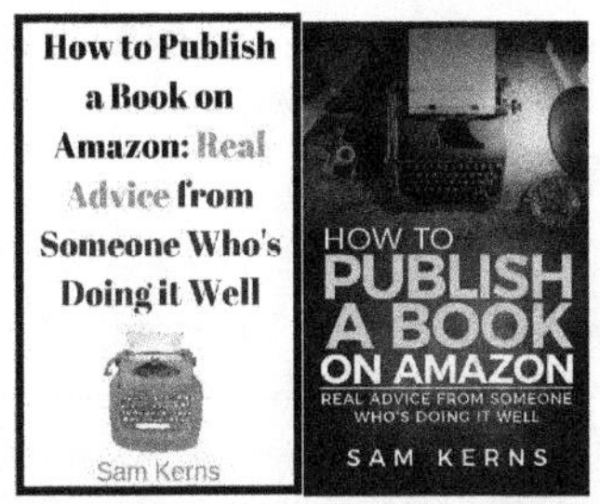

I liked the clean and crisp cover I designed on the left, but the buyers on Amazon have spoken and they prefer a more professional look for the book. But don't take this example as a one size fits all formula. My all-time bestselling book, How to Build a Writing Empire in 30 Days or Less, looks a lot like the first cover. (See it below) That's why it's so important that you step outside of yourself and ask the people who read books in your genre.

The Takeaway: Your cover is one of the key ingredients to a book that sells. If yours isn't selling, it's the first place you should look. For instance, the only change I made to *How to Publish a Book on Amazon* was the cover and it instantly began to sell. But keep in mind that it already had a lot of great reviews and is part of a well-liked series. If your book isn't consistently seen because it's too far down in the rankings, changing the cover will not give you instant results. But don't let that stop you from making sure the cover is perfect now because once you complete the steps I talk about in the following chapters, your book will be seen and your cover had better be perfect—otherwise all your hard work will be for nothing.

Next, Determine if Your Book is Still Current and Relevant

Although most authors who use the steps outlined in this book will see success, there are some books that simply can't be revived, no matter how much you try. For example, there are books for sale on Amazon right now about the Y2K bug that was predicted for the year 2000. It doesn't matter what the authors do, those books are not going to sell because they're no longer relevant.

But the problem extends to books beyond the obvious. Some books, although they are well-written and informative, need to be updated in order to get the sales going. For example, there are fiction books for sale on Amazon where the plot centers around the Y2K bug, and judging from their rankings, they're not selling many books, if any. But if the authors made some simple plot changes and updated the books, they would have a chance of selling their books again. For instance, instead of writing about the Y2K bug, they could make the plot relevant again by creating an imaginary bug and setting the plot in modern times. It wouldn't take that much to revise a book like this, and once it was finished, the author would have a current and relevant book.

And it's no different for nonfiction. Just because your book's topic is not relevant today, that doesn't mean you can't make some changes to make it current. Let's use the topic of real estate investing as an example. There are tons of seemingly good books on Amazon about the topic, but many of them are outdated. For instance, some books contain specific years in their titles and once that year has passed, people aren't likely to purchase the book because they'll (rightly) assume that the advice given in the book is outdated. In a minute, I'll show you how to use this technique the right way to instantly jump-start your sales, but for now, let's talk about how to determine whether or not your book is relevant in the minds of readers.

- If your fiction books aren't selling and you've already determined that your cover is good, or you've changed it based on the expectations of readers in your genre, you now need to figure out if the book's genre is something that people are still buying today. For example, science fiction in its purest form has given way to cyberpunk and speculative fiction and if your book is of the old standard fare, it probably isn't selling as well as it should be because readers have moved on. Another example is the romance genre. While years ago, readers wanted a heroine in distress and a guaranteed happy ending, today's readers want stronger women and a happy ever after ending isn't mandatory. If you have fiction books that aren't selling, you'll need to find out what *is* selling in your genre and tweak your book to ensure that readers will want to buy it. One of the best ways to do that is to read some of the bestselling books in your genre, and then compare them to your own book. Really take the bestselling books apart and determine what drives the plot, the characters, and the emotions readers feel. Then re-read your own book and pinpoint what's different. What do readers get from the bestselling books that they won't get from yours? Once you've determined this, make a plan to change your plot, characters, and the emotional impact of your book.

- If you write nonfiction, your goal is the same, but you should approach things differently. I'm assuming that if you write nonfiction, you are an expert in the field and can easily determine what's changed since you wrote the book. For example, if you write about real estate investing, then you know that financing options for real estate investors have changed dramatically with the introduction of the JOBS act and crowdfunding sites, along with many other significant developments in the past few years. If you haven't updated your book, readers aren't getting the newest information, and you will begin receiving reviews telling potential buyers that the information is outdated and your sales will slump. If you've written a book that is outdated, you need to update the information in it if you want people to buy it. But what about nonfiction books that aren't outdated, but the publication date makes people think they are? Let's talk about those types of books in the next section.

Evergreen Nonfiction Books

Some books are evergreen, but the publication date makes people believe that they're not current. This was my dilemma for *How to Work from Home and Make Money: 10 Proven Home-Based Business Ideas You can Start Today*. The information in the book is still current, but many books were written on the topic after I published mine that had a lot of the same business ideas in them. Then I began getting reviews saying that the book didn't contain any new ideas, and I knew I had to act. It's a good book and I didn't want to let it die, so I updated it to include some new business ideas that aren't yet in the mainstream. The book, now called *How to Work from Home and Make Money in 2017: 13 Proven Home-Based Business Ideas You can Start Today* is selling again.

Which brings me to my next point: using dates in your book's title. When people look for books in the Amazon search bar, they often use the current year to weed out old or irrelevant books. For example, when you search for any nonfiction book on Amazon, you'll often see "2017" added to the keywords in the search suggestions. So I decided to include the current year in the older books on my backlist (after updating them of course), and I saw an instant uptick in sales.

The key to this method is committing to updating your books every year, because if you don't, your books will instantly fall in the rankings as the year changes. So only use this method if you are sure that once the New Year rolls around, you will update your book and change the cover to reflect the current year. Here is a before and after of this book's cover. (I decided not to change the overall design because it has sold so many copies):

The Takeaway: Because there are so many books on Amazon, yours needs to be current and relevant if it has a chance of selling. While it may seem like a lot of work to examine the content for relevancy and timeliness, the current trends for your genre, and then committing to updating the book every year, it *will* pay off. And just think: taking these steps is a lot easier than starting from scratch and writing a new book.

Rethinking Your Book's Description

After a book cover catches the attention of someone and they click on the page to find out whether or not it's current and relevant, the next thing buyers do is read the book description to determine if it's a book they want to read. If your book description falls flat, you lose your chances of making a sale. But this is the exact area where so many authors fail.

Here's the thing to remember: your book description shouldn't tell people what the plot of a novel is, or outline the entire contents of a nonfiction book. Although at first glance, it makes sense that you would use the space for that, doing so won't help you sell books. And this is why so many authors hate writing book descriptions—they think they have to sum up their entire book in 200 words or less.

Luckily, that's just not true.

In order to use this prime Amazon real estate effectively, you've got to take a cue from the sales world and talk directly to people's area of pain. Let me first give you an example of a brief bad and good book description for both fiction and nonfiction, and then we'll talk about how to rewrite yours for your relaunch. (Keep in mind that most bestselling book descriptions have an average of about 200 words. These are intentionally shorter to make it easier to point out the good and bad aspects of them.)

Bad Fiction Book Description

Samantha was a woman in love, but the man she loved didn't even know she was alive. She tried to get his attention by making sure she always looked her best when he was around, and "accidentally" bumping into him wherever she could. But despite all of her best efforts, Samantha couldn't catch the attention of the man she believed she was destined to be with. Would Marcus finally pay attention to her, or would all her efforts be for naught?

Would you buy this book? If you're like most people, the answer is a definite no. But let's look at why you wouldn't plop down a few bucks to read the story. For starters, and most importantly, there is no emotional connection for the reader. You have an idea of what the book is about—unrequited love, which is something many people can relate to, but the description doesn't pull on your heart strings, does it? And that's the first rule of book descriptions, you have to make the reader feel the emotions necessary to make them push the buy button.

Next, the description tells you what the book is about, but it doesn't give any hints about who the characters are or what you will take away from the story. There is a question at the end of the description that is designed to pique interest, but there isn't enough there to even do that.

Let's take a look at how this book description could be better.

Good Fiction Book Description

"I wish I didn't love him so it wouldn't hurt so much."

These were the thoughts of shy but determined twenty-five year old Samantha as she arranged yet another "accidental" meeting with Marcus, the man she believed was her soul mate. But despite all her efforts, Marcus didn't even seem to know she was alive. If you've ever experienced unrequited love, you won't be able to put down this emotional tale of a woman so in love that she couldn't see the truth staring her in the face.

Scroll up and hit the buy button now to learn just how far Samantha goes to get the attention of her love—and how Marcus' reaction changes her life forever.

Buyers who read this book description will have a better idea of who Samantha is—and how the story will affect their own life. And if someone is dealing with, or has dealt with, unrequited love, they will likely hit that buy button to find out how a shy woman's persistence affected her life. With this book description the author would likely sell many more copies than if they had used the first description.

Now let's take a look at some good and bad nonfiction book descriptions.

Bad Nonfiction Book Description

Joe Smith is a freelance financial consultant who is determined to share his experience with the general public. And now he has written a book to do just that. Investing your money in the right places can be a profitable venture if you know how to do it. Buy this book now and read all about Joe's experience in the business world.

Yikes, need I say more? But if you browse Amazon, you'll see plenty of book descriptions that look a lot like that. Let's take a look at how to do it right.

Good Nonfiction Book Description

Are You One of the Millions of People Who Don't Have Enough Money to Retire?

Recent studies have shown that a great number of people haven't saved enough money to retire on. And the younger generation? They're not saving either.

Many experts are warning that social security may not be around in the near future and people shouldn't rely on it for retirement. So what will you do if you haven't saved enough? And if you're younger, what should you do now to ensure that you don't end up in this position?

Joe Smith has made his living helping people get their finances in order so they can retire comfortably, and now he brings us this explosive new book written for those on the verge of retirement—or those who are just starting out.

Don't worry about your retirement, instead, scroll up and hit the buy button to learn what steps you can take today to ensure that you won't have to work forever.

Chances are, if anyone is worried about retirement or is thinking about how to plan for it, they'll buy the book. Why? Because it directly addresses their pain point: fear of not having enough to retire on. And combine that with the fact that the book is written by a practicing expert, and you've got a winning combination. Now, most nonfiction books should have a few bullet points showing readers what they can expect to learn in the book, but I've purposefully left those out to show you the proper guts of a good book description.

Here is a list of the key points you should address in your relaunch book description:

- **Start with an impactful statement that connects with your readers.** You need to grab the reader's attention immediately, and the best way to do that is to come up with a bold statement that addresses their pain point. For example, in the fiction book description, I used the character's thoughts to connect with readers who feel or have felt the same emotions. And in the nonfiction example, I used the fear of not having enough money to retire. In both instances, the statements would help readers identify with the book.

- **Sell, don't tell.** You should tell the reader just enough to make them understand what the book is about and pique their curiosity. Don't use your book description to describe your book in full. Think of it like a movie trailer. After watching one, do you know the entire plot, or just enough to make you want to go and see it? You need to use the same technique for your book description.

- **Don't be boring.** Boring and stuffy don't sell. No matter how much of an expert you are, you need to relate to your audience. Unless you are writing academic books, you'll need to talk to readers as if you're having a conversation with them. On that note, many people say you should write in the third person for your book description, but that's a rule I don't adhere to. My goal is to connect with my readers and I write in first person to forge that connection.

- **Ask for the sale.** Countless studies have shown that people are much more likely to make a purchase if they're asked, so be sure to ask the reader to buy your book. You can do this any way you choose, just don't be obnoxious in your call to action. Just a simple, "scroll up and buy the book" seems to work just fine.

The Takeaway: **After your cover, rewriting your book description is one of the most important things you can do for a successful relaunch. It has been estimated that a new book is released on Amazon every 5 minutes, which means you need to do all you can to convince readers that your book is the one they've been looking for. Take a hard look at your existing book description and put yourself in your reader's shoes. Can you connect with it? Does it make you want to read more? Does the author appear credible? Until you can answer yes to all of these questions, you'll need to keep working on it.

A Word About Editing

What I'm about to tell you in this chapter defies just about anything you've ever read on the subject. If you listen to most self-publishing gurus, they'll tell you that you have to spend hundreds, or even thousands of dollars to have your book professionally edited. But I'm a business man, and I have to tell you, for most people, that just doesn't make sense. Here's the way I see things:

The average person will make just over $200 on their book. Now, before you panic, I need to tell you that you don't *have* to be average. I believe the people that make so little money publish a book, maybe run a promotion or two, and then move on and forget about it. If you've read any of my other books, especially *How to Publish a Book on Amazon*, you'll realize that it's not necessary to be "average" in this industry.

But even those who make over $200 on their book probably can't justify spending thousands of dollars on editing. That's why I don't do it.

You see, I believe you should be paid for your hard work. Writing a book isn't easy, and it just doesn't make sense to me to spend a lot of money upfront only to break even on the back end. In fact, I think it's reckless for people to advise it. They do so on the premise that if you're going to have a bestselling book, it needs to be perfect. That's fine, but here's my theory. I release my books after editing them as best as I can by myself. I've had some great successes, and some books that haven't sold well, but none of them have been affected by the fact that there may be a typo or two in them. Have I had some dings in my reviews due to a few typos? Sure, but most of my reviews are positive and I know people are greatly helped by my books.

Please don't misunderstand me and think I'm telling you not to re-edit your book if it needs it. When you relaunch your book, you should do all you can to improve it, and if you have a great number of reviews talking about the grammar mistakes in your book, you will need to do something about it. Here is my editing process—if you have the skills, you should at the minimum do this for your book before you relaunch it:

- Use a software program like ProWritingAid to catch any glaring mistakes in your manuscript. You can use the program for free if you edit small chunks at a time, or you can pay $40 a year for the premium version.
- Print out the book and read it from start to finish, marking any changes that need to be made. Make the changes in your digital document, and print it out again. Do this several times until you don't find any more errors.
- Print your document again, and this time read it out loud. Doing so will help you catch any errors you previously missed. Again make the needed corrections and print it out again.
- Now you'll need to read the document backwards. Start with the last sentence of the manuscript, and read each one before that. To catch the most errors, read the sentences out loud.
- Correct the errors that you find again, and then give your manuscript to any friends and family members who are willing to help. Ask each one to contact you with any mistakes they find, and then make the corrections.
- If you have a mailing list, do what I do and ask anyone who is willing to read your book in exchange for an honest review to keep a list of typos that they find and email them to you. If you haven't yet built your mailing list, don't worry. I will tell you exactly how to do it in a future chapter.

- Put a note in your books asking your readers to always contact you when they find a grammatical error. My faithful readers are wonderful at letting me know when they find one, and as soon as they do, I correct the manuscript and republish it immediately. I can't tell you how grateful I am every time I receive one of these thoughtful emails.

If you take all of these steps, your book should be edited and ready for publication.

I'd like to make a personal note here: I am editing this book as an evacuee from Hurricane Harvey, so I ask that you forgive me if you find errors. In fact, if you do, please send me a quick note at samkernsbooks@gmail.com and let me know about it so I can correct it immediately. *My family and I are fine, but our home suffered a lot damage and my editing eyes are a tad bit distracted. I would also like to give a shout out to Amazon who graciously allowed me to extend the release of the book due to the hurricane.

Well, that brings us to the conclusion of this chapter. Reevaluating your book is at the foundation of your relaunch because you need to determine why it hasn't been selling. By looking at these key elements of your book, you should be able to pinpoint the problem. And just to make it easier, there is a simple worksheet on the next page that will help you hone in and focus on the key areas of your book.

The Takeaway: Editing your book is important, but it's not realistic for most authors to spend thousands, or even hundreds of dollars paying someone to do it. Take the steps outlined above, and if after relaunching your book, it climbs to the top 100 on Amazon, by all means, spend your money and have it done professionally! (Note: Some people will have to pay for professional editing. If you don't have the skills and your book has serious grammatical errors, you will have no choice but to hire an editor.) If you do need to hire one, go to reedsy.com and check out their list of qualified freelancers.

Worksheet: Create an Improvement Road Map for Your Book

Here's a step-by-step roadmap that breaks down chapter one and helps you identify your book's weaknesses and improve them.

Analyze Your Book Cover

Your book cover is the first impression you'll make, so it needs to be perfect. Here's how to ensure your cover is the right one for your book:

1. Look at the top 20 books in your genre and make note of the:

   a) Colors
   b) Fonts
   c) Style/Theme

2. Then compare it to yours. What's different? Don't copy these covers, but make sure yours fits in your genre, otherwise readers won't recognize your book as one they want to read.

3. Have a new cover designed or create one yourself. Make several versions of the cover using different fonts and colors.

4. Next, take a survey of likely readers to determine which one they like most. The one with the most votes will probably sell better.

Do Some Genre Research

In order to be successful as an author, you need to keep up with current trends in your genre. That's true whether you write fiction, nonfiction, children's books or anything else. And if you find that your book is outdated, you'll need to revise it in order to make it current. If for some reason, you haven't kept up with the trends, Writing-World.com has compiled an excellent list of writers organizations for every genre that will help you get up to speed.

Here are the questions you'll need to ask yourself:

1. Does your book contain any outdated material that needs to be updated?

2. Do you need to add information to the book? For instance, I added 3 chapters to *How to Work from Home and Make Money*.

3. If you've written a novel, do you need to rewrite any scenes that date the book? For instance, do any of your characters use pay phones instead of cell phones? (If you've written a period novel, of course this wouldn't affect you.)

4. If you include links in your books, check them to make sure they're still active and working. The same goes for any prices you quote or other things that can change over time.

5. Think about adding the current year to your title, and then including the line "Revised and updated for (Year)" in your book description. But only do this is you're committed to updating your book every year.

Change Your Book Description

Now it's time to re-write your book description so readers will connect with your book and want to buy it. Do this by:

1. Starting with a bold statement that connects to readers on an emotional level. Play to their hopes, fears, wishes, and longings.

2. Citing any professional accolades that you have. If you practice in the industry you're writing about, be sure to include it, and if you've won any awards for your book, that should be front and center.

3. Including just enough information to make them want to read more. Remember, structure your book description like a movie trailer. Tell them enough to get them excited enough to buy the book to keep reading.

4. Asking them to buy the book. This one simple tactic will pay off in increased sales.

Think About Re-Editing Your Book

No book is perfect, but yours should be as good as you can get it. If you've received numerous reviews about the grammar in your book, re-edit it using the steps outlined above. And if you don't have the skills or patience to do that, you'll need to hire someone to do the job for you.

Chapter Two: Rearrange Your Book's Categories Using My Lift-Off Strategy

Now that your book is updated, edited, and you've decided on a new cover—or an old one with a few tweaks—it's time to think about which categories your book should be in. If you're like most authors, your book has sat in the same categories since it was first published, and I'm here to tell you that's a big, big mistake. In fact, choosing the right categories is so important to a books' success that I tend to change mine every couple of months.

But before I tell you how to choose the right categories for your book, let me tell you why it's so important.

How Amazon Categories Work

As you know, there are millions of books published on Amazon, and every day more are added. The reason this matters to you is that the number one thing you can do to sell more books on Amazon is to make sure your book is seen. And the best way to do that? To put it in the right categories.

Amazon organizes its millions of book in categories and customers use these categories to search for books. For example, if someone were looking for a book about how to start a small business, they would likely look in the entrepreneurship/small business category. The books that are visible in that category, particularly the top 20, will be seen and because of that, they will sell the most copies.

Choosing the right categories for your book is important, but that's particularly true when you're conducting a relaunch. Look at it this way, if your book has sat in the same category for some time and hasn't sold, it's time to change things up. And I believe I have designed a great formula for doing just that. I call it my Lift Off Strategy because it has worked for me time and time again. Here's how it works:

Use the Lift Off Strategy to Sell More Books

If you've chosen the right cover, written a good book that's current and relevant for its genre, and crafted a book description that makes people want to buy it, your next step is to position the book where people can find it. Here's how I use this strategy to relaunch my books and keep them selling.

Step One: Ignore the Suggestions in the KDP Setup Page

When most people go to change their book's category, they go into the KDP setup page and choose one of the categories listed there. But that is the last thing you should do. Amazon only lists a fraction of the available categories there, and most of them are so broad that your book will never have a chance of being seen. Instead, you'll need to do some detective work and scout out the best categories for your book.

Step Two: Find Suitable Categories for Your Book

Amazon isn't very forthcoming about their categories and I've found the best way to identify them is to spend a few hours on the site looking at similar books. Start by finding the bestselling books in your genre and then going to each page and looking at which categories they're listed in. Make a list of all that fit your book, keeping track of the sales rank of the #1 and #20 book in the category. For example, if I were looking for categories for a book about small business, I would look in the broad category of Business, then find all of the books similar to mine. I would go page by page and look at the categories those books are listed under. I would then write down the categories, the rank of each book and what kind of placement that rank gave them in the category.

By the time I'd looked at 20 books, I would have a list of categories and a good idea what rank I would need to make the first page (top 20) of each one. Let me give you an example.

This book hasn't released yet, but when it does, I have identified the following possible categories to list it in.

Kindle Store>Kindle eBooks>Reference>Writing, Research & Publishing Guides>Publishing & Books>Authorship. The number 1 book in this competitive category is 2,800 while the book holding the #20 spot has ranking of 33,000.

Kindle Store>Kindle eBooks>Reference>Writing, Research & Publishing Guides>Nonfiction. The number 1 book in this category has a sales rank of just over 7,000, and the book that has the #20 spot has a ranking of almost 110,000. Obviously, this category would be easier to rank in the top 20.

Kindle Store> Kindle eBooks>Business & Money>Marketing & Sales>Advertising>Writing Skills. This category's number 1 book has a ranking of 7,700 and the book that holds the number 20 spot has a ranking of 122,000. Again, this would be an easy one to break into. (This book has already reached the #1 New Release status in this category—see below.)

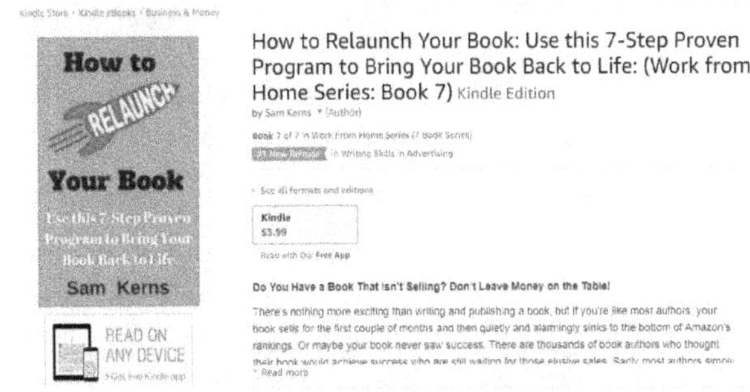

Step Three: Select Your Categories Based on a Sales-Driven Philosophy

Now that you have a list of possible categories, you should look for the one that would be the easiest to reach the top 20, and the one that would be difficult, but possible. If your book has sold in the past and you're relaunching it in hopes of reviving it, it should be easy to identify the categories you think you would achieve this based on prior sales. But if your book has never sold, you'll need to do some guessing. How do you do that?

I can't guarantee success, but if you do everything I outline in this book, I would be shocked if your book didn't reach a minimum of 100,000 in the rankings and it should reach much higher than that. Most books will reach a minimum of a 30,000 ranking if you faithfully follow these steps, and that should make your book visible in most categories.

The reason you want to choose an easy category and a difficult one is because the easy category will drive sales to the more difficult one. Here's how it works:

Fewer people look in the more obscure categories, but your will book will be ranked higher in them, possibly even achieving bestseller status. For example, when I launch this book, I fully expect to reach bestseller status in the Kindle Store>Kindle eBooks>Reference>Writing, Research & Publishing Guides>Nonfiction category if I choose that one. And once I have that orange tag by my book, it will not only grab the attention of more buyers, but Amazon will begin promoting it. Suddenly, it will appear in the Hot New Releases category and that will drive even more sales. All of these "extra" sales will cause the ranking to go up, which will give me better placement in the more difficult category, where more people look for books like mine.

Do you see why categories are so darn important?

Keep in mind that some of Amazon's categories require that you use certain keywords when you set up your book. For a complete listing of those categories and the required keywords, go to Amazon's help page "Selecting Browse Categories." And in addition to entering the keywords on your setup page, you should try to include them in your book description and title if you can do it without sounding spammy.

I need to take a minute here and address a current trend that's happening. Some authors are choosing completely irrelevant categories so they can ensure they receive the bestseller tag by their book, but I wholeheartedly disagree with this approach. Here's why. If I were to release this book and reach bestseller status in the Childhood Art, category, what do you think it would accomplish? It certainly wouldn't bring in buyers from that category because shoppers looking in that category aren't looking for a book about how to relaunch a book.

And even more importantly, people don't like to be gamed, and when I see a book reach bestseller status in a completely unrelated category, it raises a red flag for me. Is the author really that desperate? Why can't they reach bestselling status in a relevant category? Are they trying to trick people into believing the book is more popular than it really is? Is there something wrong with the book that they have to resort to such dishonest tactics?

Is it just me, or is there a better way of doing things? Personally, I choose relevant categories and use the steps outlined in this book to reach bestselling status. It's worked so far and I believe my readers appreciate the fact that I release good books in an honest and straightforward way.

Finally, keep in mind that you can change your book's categories any time you want. So if you choose one for your relaunch and don't make the top 20 for it, simply go back to your research notes and find an easier category. You can—and should—tweak your categories as often as it takes to ensure that you're in the top 20 in all of them.

The Takeaway: The right categories are like a gold mine for your book. But be smart about it and choose a *relevant* category that's easy to break into the top 20 so it will help propel your book to the top, and a more popular category so that when your ranking rises, it will be seen by all the buyers who look there for books like yours.

Chapter Three: Reviews can Help Relaunch Your Book—Here's How to Get Them

Ah, reviews, the bane of every self-published writer's existence. We live and die by them, don't we? Get a good one and we walk around on cloud 9 for the rest of the day, but God forbid someone leaves us a bad one.

But as much as we rely on reviews to tell us how we're doing in the eyes of our readers, book buyers rely on them to decide whether or not to make a purchase. That's why it's so important to get as many good reviews for your book as you can before you relaunch it. In an age of social proof, people simply don't like to make purchases without first seeing that other people have bought the product and are happy with it, and it's no different for books.

But ask any indie author, and they will tell you that getting readers to leave a review for their books is almost more difficult than writing the book.

Luckily, there are some things you can do to get reviews, and the rest of the steps that I outline in the upcoming chapters will require you to have them. So don't skip over this chapter, thinking that you can relaunch your book without a good number of reviews, because if you do, you won't see the kind of success I'm talking about.

The Top 9 Ways to Get Book Reviews

Before I list the top 9 ways to get book reviews, I need to clarify something: it's hard work. And it takes time—lots of it. But you'll need a minimum of ten solid reviews before you can even think about relaunching your book, and more would be better. The more reviews you have, the better your chances will be at scoring quality promotions, and convincing buyers that your book is worth their money. But like I said, prepare to work for them because they're not easy to get.

Ask People You Know

Let me quickly clarify what I mean. Amazon doesn't allow your friends and family to leave reviews for your book, and if they find out that they have, they will delete the review. Even worse, if it happens more than once, they may even suspend your author account. So when I tell you to ask people you know to leave reviews for your book, I'm not talking about asking your mom or your best friend.

But the people in your inner circle know people you've never met, and they are the people you should seek reviews from. For example, the woman your wife works with might agree to read your book and leave an honest review, as could the babysitter who looks after your best friend's kids. The possibilities are endless and reaching out beyond your circles is a quick way to get reviews for your book.

Hang out on Goodreads

When looking for reviews, you'll need to find the places readers gather, and for that, you can't do better than Goodreads. If you haven't already, set up an author account there and then begin looking at all of the groups. There are groups for just about every genre, and if you politely ask for honest reviews in exchange for a free book, you'll likely get a few takers. Just read the rules because readers there tend to get cross when authors become too promotional.

Have a Free Day

When you give away a lot of books, you're bound to get some reviews in return. The trick here is to hold the free day after you've revamped your book, but before you relaunch it. If your book is enrolled in KDP Select (and it should be because it dramatically improves your rankings), then you can take advantage of the 5-day free day promotion and give away as many books as you can. This will result in some reviews, depending on how many you give away.

In addition to the KDP Select free days, you can enroll your book on Instafreebie where it will be given away for the period of time you select. You can sign up for a free 30 day trial period and give away books in hopes of getting some reviews.

If you choose this route to get reviews, you'll have to do it early enough in the process because many of the promotion sites won't run a discounted book if it's been listed as free recently.

Ask for Them in Your Book

Another great way to get reviews is to ask your readers for them. I include a request for reviews at the end of all my books, and many readers have told me that it caused them to leave a review. Remember, it doesn't hurt to ask, and you're likely to increase your reviews if you do. Be sure to make things easy for your readers by including a link that will take them directly to the review page. And to all of you who have left reviews for my books, thank you! And for those of you who haven't, I have a special picture just for you. I'm just saying…

Find Book Reviewers on Amazon

Where's the best place to find book reviewers? Where they hang out, of course. And the number one place book lovers love to be is on Amazon, which is why I always start there when looking for book reviews. And when you're going to relaunch a book, this is one of the quickest ways to get them—but I must warn you, it will take a few hours to find reviewers using this method.

Start by creating a spreadsheet with columns for the book title, name of the person you're going to ask for a review, their email address, the date you contacted them, and if they agree, the date they reviewed your book.

Now begin by typing your keywords into the Amazon search bar and making a list of all the books on the first page. Then go to each one of them and look at their reviews. Narrow down the results you see by clicking on "All reviews" and then "Positive reviews." Now, you'll need to click on each reviewer's name, which will take you to their profile page. On that page, you'll see a "See more" link, and when you click it, it will show the reviewer's email address if they've chosen to share it. If it's there, add the information to your spreadsheet.

You will need to do this until you have at least 100 names, and that's going to take some time. The general rule of thumb is that you'll get about a 10 percent response rate, which means you would get 10 reviews for every 100 requests you send out, but sometimes you'll get lucky and get more than that.

Now that you have all the names, you'll need to make contact with them and ask them for a review. Here's the message I typically send out:

Hi,

My name is Sam Kerns and I noticed that you left a review on Amazon for (name of book they left a review for). I have written a similar book that I think you might enjoy. Would you consider reading my book for free in exchange for an honest review? If so, please just let me know which format you'd like it in and I'll send it right away.

I'm running a promotion for this book on (date), and would greatly appreciate it if you could leave the review by then.

Best to you and yours,

Sam

If you don't have all of those file types for your book, head on over to Draft2Digital and set up your book. After it's set up (you don't have to publish it in order to set it up), you can download all of the file types.

Use Software that Does the Same Thing

If you're one of those rare indie authors who have a lot of money to spare, you can purchase software that will do all of the above in a fraction of the time it would take you to do it yourself. The software is called Book Review Targeter and for a mere $197, it will find all those names and email address for you. The software pricing has recently changed, and is now billed at about $16 per month with a one-year commitment.

If that's a little rich for you, there is a less expensive alternative called Book Razor. This service will find 100 reviewers for you and then provide them to you on a spreadsheet ready to go for about $50. There are different price plans that will give more or fewer reviewer names and contact information. It will save you hours of work, and as a bonus, you'll be able to build relationships with the reviewers and ask them to leave reviews on future books as you release them. I've used this service myself and highly recommend them.

Ask Your List for Reviews

If you don't already have an email list, you'll need to immediately take the steps to build one because you'll need one if you're going to succeed as an indie author. I'll show you two of the easiest and fastest ways to do this in an upcoming chapter. But for this section, I'm going to assume that you already have one.

A few weeks before you relaunch your book, send out an email asking your list to leave reviews for it. Be sure to offer the book for free for those who haven't yet read it, and be sure to let them know the date of the relaunch so they can leave the review before then. It's a simple way to get the reviews you need without a lot of effort, and your readers will be thrilled to be a part of your relaunch. I can't tell you how good it does my heart to hear from my readers every time I send out an email. It just reaffirms that what I'm doing is making a difference and there is simply no substitute for that.

Contact Book Bloggers and Ask for a Review

Book bloggers are people who read books and then talk to their audience about those books, giving their opinions about them. A blogger with a large following holds significant influence over their followers and can not only result in reviews for your book, but sales. But a lot of authors approach them asking for reviews, and if you're going to pursue this method, you'll need to stand out from the crowd.

First, it should go without saying that your book needs to be well-written, polished, and the cover should look professional. If you've come this far in the relaunch process, you've already nailed those aspects of your book.

Next, you'll need to carefully think about how to approach each blogger instead of sending out mass emails that all sound alike. To catch a blogger's attention, start off your letter talking about a review they've written, or telling them why you believe they would be interested in reviewing your book. Remember, these people get a lot of requests, and it's your job to differentiate yourself and your book.

Here's a brief list of steps you can take to get the best results.

- Look for a book blogger that reviews books in your genre. Most reputable sites list book bloggers by category. Go to bookbloggerdirectory.wordpress.com, Bookbloggerslist.com, and The Indieview.com to find book bloggers who read books like yours.
- Look at their blog and get a feel for the types of books they like and what they don't like about books in your genre. This will ensure that your book is a good match for the blogger. Also pay attention to the reviews they write and make some notes so you can personalize your request.
- Read the submission guidelines for each blogger. They will all have preferences and you need to make sure you follow them perfectly. For example, some bloggers only want to read a print copy while others ask that you allow them 2 or more months to leave a review.
- Send a personalize email to the blogger. Here's your chance to shine. Send them an email that is succinct, personalized, and makes them want to read your book. Remember to keep it short while including all of the pertinent details.
- If you haven't heard back from the blogger within a few weeks, follow up with another note.
- Once a blogger agrees to read your book, send it to them in the format they prefer and ask them for an estimated timeline and then sit back and wait for their review. Be sure to request that they not only leave a review for your book on their website, but also on Amazon.
- Once their review is live, you should send the blogger a thank you note, even if it's not the review you'd hoped for. Then, you can share it on your social media platforms or website. Some book bloggers like to review books by the same

author, so if you got a positive review, be sure and send a request for your next book, too.

Pay for Book Reviews

If you haven't achieved results with the above suggestions, you can always pay for reviews, but I have to warn you, it will cost a lot of money. Now, I'm not talking about hiring one of the questionable review providers on places like Fiverr, but legitimate sites that won't get you in trouble with Amazon. Sites like Kirkusreviews.com, Bookreporter.com and Bookpage.com all offer review services for indie authors and are perfectly acceptable to the powers at be at the Zon. These places don't guarantee that they'll accept your book for review, but if they do, it looks awfully good on your book page. Keep in mind that submitting your book to one of these review sites will typically cost hundreds of dollars, and you can't guarantee that the review will be in your favor.

Finally, you will eventually get organic reviews from people who buy and read your book. Once I have enough reviews to promote my book, I typically just rely on these organic reviews to come naturally.

Now that you've analyzed every aspect of your book and made it as good as you can, it's time to move on the next step: ensuring that your relaunch leads to other sales from your backlist.

The Takeaway: **Getting reviews for your book takes a lot of work and patience, but once you have them, you'll have a better chance at succeeding with your book relaunch. Commit to spending a few hours to contact the people you need to get at least 10 reviews for your books.**

Chapter Four: Put Your Internal Marketing Techniques in Place to Increase Sales from Your Backlist

Now that your book is new and shiny and the best it can be, let's talk about a few other things you can do to increase the sales of the other books in your backlist. But for those of you who don't know what a backlist is, let's go back to basics for a moment.

What's a Backlist and Why is It so Important?

In its simplest definition, a backlist is made up of all the prior books you've published. For instance, if you're about to relaunch the third book you've written, you have two other books in your back list, and if you're reading this book, chances are they aren't selling well either.

So, let's fix that.

Backlists are important for both fiction and non-fiction alike because when someone reads your book and likes it, they're likely to purchase other books that you've written. And if you relaunch your book correctly, it will not only revive the relaunched book, but the others in your backlist as well.

In fact, in order to achieve the best sales results during your relaunch, you should consider updating the content and book covers for all the books in your backlist. For example, when I relaunched *How to Work from Home and Make Money*, I updated a few of the older titles in my backlist.

If you don't have a backlist and have only written one book, you might want to wait until you've released at least one more before relaunching your book. The same holds true if you write in more than one pen name and only have one book published under each name. This is not mandatory of course, but if you want to reap the most benefits from the relaunch, you should definitely relaunch your book when you have more than one book for people to buy.

But there's a trick to doing it right, and that's what I want to talk about here. *There are two things you must have in place before you schedule your relaunch.*

Create a Series to Increase Your Book Sales

There are many studies that show books in a series sell better than those that stand alone, but what does that really mean? And can you create a series even if you don't write serial fiction or publish nonfiction books that don't link together? The answer is not only yes you can do that, but you *have* to do it in order to reap the most sales from your relaunch—and lifetime sales.

Here's why: Amazon is full of tempting books for buyers and those authors who make it easy for buyers to find the books on their backlist will sell more books. It's a simple fact, and luckily it's not difficult to put your backlist in front of buyers.

Take a quick look at one of my book pages and see how I've put together my series. I named it the Work from Home series, and it includes books on everything from publishing, branding a small business, starting a food business, and my next book will be about why it's so important to develop an entrepreneurial mindset in order to succeed in life—and how to do it.

It can be argued that all the books in my series are geared toward those people who want to work for themselves, and that's true, but there's another reason why they are all included in a series. Scroll down the page a little until you get to the Books in this Series carousel. There, you'll find every book I've written to date and guess what? So will the people who are browsing for a book to buy. For example, if someone lands on my *How to Work from Home and Make Money* book and decides not to buy it, they may then see *How to Start a Home-Based Food Business* and decide it's the right book for them.

In addition to increasing random purchases, people who like my books can find my entire backlist easily and my sales show it. Let me give you an example of why this is so important. I put together a boxed set titled The Writer's Toolkit, which includes books 2 and 5 in the series, but Amazon doesn't allow boxed sets to be linked to a series. The result? I hardly sell any of the boxed set because no one knows about it. And that's a boxed set that include 2 bestselling books!

You can create a series for nonfiction books by identifying a common theme in the books and then creating a title that ties them together like my Work from Home series. There are no limits to this—you can somehow tie together any books you want with the right title. And fiction books are no different, even if the books aren't part of an ongoing plotline. For example, my good friend April Geremia writes standalone books, but still includes them all in her Souls of the Sea series.

How to Turn Your Books into a Series

Even if you've published your books as standalones, you'll want to group them together into a series before you relaunch your book so you'll reap the most sales from your effort. Luckily, doing this is simple, but it will take some time for Amazon to create your series carousel so be sure to plan ahead. Here are the steps you'll need to take:

- Go to your bookshelf on KDP and look for the Series section just below the Book Title section. Enter the series name and then the series number. When you looked at my series page, you noticed that the books are numbered 1-7. I number mine as I release them, but you can put your books in any order you want. Save your changes and exit KDP.

- As soon as you've entered all of your books in the series, go to your Amazon Central account and click Help in the top right corner. Then look to the left column and click on Contact Us. Answer the questions and select the option that allows you to contact them via email. In an email, let them know that you've set up a series and request that it's linked together as soon as possible so you can run your promotion. You can also choose to call them, but I've found that sending an email is sufficient. It's taken as long as a month to have a book added to my series—and at times I've had to contact them more than once—so be sure you do this step as soon as possible so it doesn't delay your relaunch. (And whatever you do, don't relaunch your book until you've taken this step—no matter how impatient you are!)

Once you've completed this step, you'll have at your disposal another great way to increase the sales of your backlist. Let's talk about that now.

The Greatest Internal Marketing Move You Can Make

Do you want to sell more books? There is a technique you can use that will bring in sales every month without you having to lift a finger. In fact, it's so simple I can't believe more people aren't doing it. Let me show you how it works.

Flip to the back of this book and you will see a catalogue of my books. I dedicate at least one page to each book and give readers a short summary of the books, as well as a picture of the book's cover. At the end of the summary, I provide a link that takes the reader directly to the book's page on Amazon where readers can purchase it if they choose—or they can browse my other books in the series carousel if they prefer.

I include this catalogue in every one of my books, and in addition, I use the same kind of links in my "Books by Sam Kerns" page at the front of the book. Talk about making it easy for people to buy other books in my series! And I know it works because I use shortened URLs at sites like Bitly.com that allow me to track the number of times someone clicks on them. In other words, I know exactly how many people click on the links to my books and that's how I know this simple step leads to additional sales each and every month. But keep in mind that to get the most benefits from this technique, your books should be grouped together in a series like we talked about above.

Just imagine, when you relaunch your book, doing these two simple things will exponentially increase the total number of books you sell—without any extra effort from you apart from the initial set up.

We've got one more step to talk about before we get into the specifics of launching your book: building your email list. I promised you earlier that I would show you 2 ways to do this quickly and easily, and that's what we'll talk about in the next chapter. Are you ready? Let's get to it!

The Takeaway: Internal marketing is almost as important as running promotions and other external marketing techniques, but it has one advantage: it's completely passive. In other words, once you set up your internal marketing, you won't have to do anything else to reap the sales from it. Set up your books a series and then link to them all in your books and you'll gain more sales from your book relaunch. It's as simple as that!

Chapter Five: How to Use Your Book Relaunch to Build Your Email List

You're going to a lot of trouble to make your book relaunch as good as you can, so why not take the opportunity to take advantage of all the focus that will be on your book and use it to increase the size of your mailing list? (Or start one.) Developing a well-established and loyal mailing list is one of the best things you can do for your author career, and a book relaunch is the perfect time to start one or increase your current list.

The system I'm about to tell you about is so simple, yet so effective, I am shocked that as far as I can tell, no one else is doing it. Here it is in a nutshell: I give away my books for free in exchange for a review to everyone on my mailing list. In fact, if you've ever read any of my books, you've seen this in both the front and back of my books:

**Read my books for
FREE by signing up for
my mailing list! Click
here or go to
RainMakerPress.com**

And if you're already a part of my mailing list, you know that when I'm about to launch a new book, I'll send you an email asking if you will read it for free and then leave an honest review for it on Amazon.

People, I'm telling you, this is the fastest way to build an email list that exists. But here's what I don't do. I don't constantly bombard my list with sales promotions or other cheesy offers because I value them and consider our relationship a two-way street. I only contact them when I'm about to launch a book, or when another author lets me know about a free book or something else that I think they would appreciate.

And it works. I built my list rapidly and my open rate is way above average. In addition, I have the privilege of exchanging personal emails with the people on my list and even get to follow their careers and hear about their successes!

Now I understand that some of you may want to build an email list to sell them stuff, and I'm not disparaging that business model, but it's just not how I choose to interact with my list. But if that's your goal, this method would likely work for you as well. Keep in mind that in order to sell to an email list, you must first establish trust and continuously offer them something of value—and this model will satisfy both of those needs.

Because your book will be downloaded hundreds, or even thousands of times, everyone who reads it will see your offer. And if they like your writing style and your book, chances are, they will sign up to your email list.

But where should you send them to enter their email address? I've got some thoughts on that, too.

How to Create a Landing Page for Less than $8 a Month

There are all sorts of expensive services that offer funnels or streamlined website pages so people can sign up for your mailing list, but unless you're trying to sell them something, all you really need is a landing page where they can enter their email address. And while it's possible to create these landing pages for free on sites like Wordpress.org, you'll have to have a little tech know-how in order to create a professional looking site.

But if you want to do it the easy way—and don't mind spending about 8 bucks a month— you can create a landing page that will impress your visitors. I use Squarespace for mine, and easily created a page that converts very well. In fact, if you haven't seen what you can get for only 8 bucks a month, check it out at RainMakerPress.com.

On my landing page, I offer a brief description of my latest book, along with a reminder that if they sign up for my list, they'll get to read it for free in exchange for an honest review. And if I ever want to expand my offerings, I can easily add pages and an online store to my site.

If you think this is the right avenue for you, SquareSpace allows you to sign up for a free trial so you can play around and create your perfect landing page.

That's the first method I use to rapidly build my email list, but there's another step you can take that will cause a lot of people to sign up. And although it's not related to your book launch. I'll mention it here while we're on the subject.

Use Instafreebie to Add More People to Your List

Instafreebie.com is a site where readers can go to download free books in exchange for their email address. The site is simple for authors to use, and it even allows you try it out for free for 30 days. In fact, it's so simple that if you upload your book you'll likely get a few hundred people to sign up to your list by the time the 30 day free trial period is over.

There are two schools of thought about this mailing list building method. Some people don't like it because some of the people who sign up are only looking for a free book, and will unsubscribe as soon as they get it. Others see the benefit, despite the fact that not everyone who signs up will become a loyal member of a list. I fall into the latter school of thought.

I first experienced Instafreebie when another author asked me to be a part of a multi-author giveaway they were hosting. I agreed and uploaded my book to Instafreebie, and was shocked at how quickly people began signing up, even before the promotion began. By the end of the promotion, I had more than 500 new people on my list. And while 20-30 of them unsubscribed after my first email, I still retained 430 email subscribers from that promotion, all of whom remain on my list today.

All in all, it's not a bad deal. But keep in mind that you'll have to time this right because you won't be able to do it during your book relaunch. If you did, Amazon may price match your book to free, and that would kill your relaunch. You also can't run an instafreebie promotion before your relaunch because many promotional sites won't feature a book that's been priced at free within the past few months. So tuck this knowledge away and use it to build your email list after you relaunch your book.

The Takeaway: Building your email list is one of the most important things you can do for your author career. And while it takes time and patience, as long as you have a good foundation, it can be done. Lay your foundation by creating a unique but simple landing page, offering your books for free in exchange for honest reviews (or any other giveaway you believe will attract email subscribers), and then use Instafreebie to quickly add more people to your list once your relaunch is complete.

What's Next?

If you've faithfully completed all the steps I've talked about, you're ready to relaunch your book. But just like every other step in the process, there is a distinct way to approach it if you want to get the best results. Let's talk about that now.

Chapter Six: Here is the Exact Formula I Used to Make My Almost Two-Year-Old Book a Bestseller

Now that you've done all you can to revamp and update your book—and those in your backlist—it's time to plan your relaunch. Remember, Amazon typically takes some time to group books in a series, so I recommend waiting until you see the series carousel on your book's pages before you proceed to this step, even if you have an estimated date from Amazon. (Those dates tend to come and go, and you can't always rely on them.)

Because of the way Amazon's algorithms work, you'll need to plan your relaunch in a way that tells Amazon your book is capable of selling in the long term. And the way to do that is to ensure that you have sales coming in over a long period of time—not just the day of your promotion.

And that will take some planning.

You will have to work with the promotional sites to organize the dates for each promotion you run so that your book stays up in the rankings for some time. And that can be tricky because some of them take a week to let you know whether or not your request is accepted or denied, and if your requested date isn't available, you'll have to do some rearranging with the other sites. And then there is the possibility that the promotional site won't even accept your book, which will result in your having to reconfigure your entire relaunch.

So plan on spending some time on this step communicating with the promotion sites and adjusting your schedule until it's just right.

Let me start out by showing you the ranking for *How to Work from Home and Make Money* before I relaunched it.

File Size: 1616 KB
Print Length: 149 pages
Simultaneous Device Usage: Unlimited
Publisher: Rainmaker Press (March 30, 2016)
Publication Date: March 30, 2016
Sold by: Amazon Digital Services LLC
Language: English
ASIN: B01CTMI7R4
Text-to-Speech: Enabled
X-Ray: Not Enabled
Word Wise: Enabled
Lending: Enabled
Screen Reader: Supported
Enhanced Typesetting: Enabled
Amazon Best Sellers Rank: #200,853 Paid in Kindle Store (See Top 100 Paid in Kindle Store)
#156 in Kindle Store > Kindle eBooks > Business & Money > Job Hunting & Careers > **Job Hunting**
#193 in Kindle Store > Kindle eBooks > Business & Money > Entrepreneurship & Small Business > **Starting a Business**
#261 in Kindle Store > Kindle eBooks > Business & Money > Entrepreneurship & Small Business > **Home-Based**

As you can see, it sat at a sad 200, 853 and was number 156 in the smallest category and a depressing 261 in the largest category. Not a pretty picture is it?

But here's what it looked like after the relaunch:

How to Work From Home and Make Money in 2017: 13 Proven Home-Based Businesses You Can Start Today (Work from Home Series: Book 1) Kindle Edition

by Sam Kerns (Author)

27 customer reviews

Book 1 of 7 in Work From Home Series (7 Book Series)

#1 Best Seller in Starting a Business

> See all formats and editions

Kindle
$0.00 kindleunlimited

This title and over 1 million more available with Kindle Unlimited
$0.99 to buy

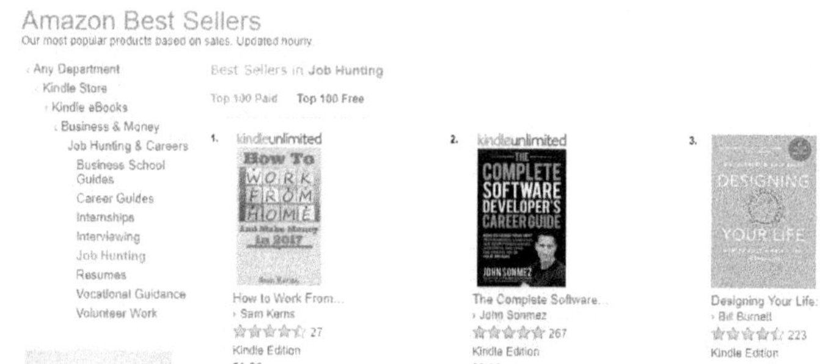

Yep, it made the bestseller list in both categories and hit 1,323 overall in the Amazon store, even though I ran into a major snag during the relaunch. We'll talk about that in minute, but first I want to show you the method I used to relaunch my book.

Day One and Two

For the first day, I chose Buck Books for the promotion because I tend to get between 40 and 60 book sales every time I use them. It's not enough to get to number one in the big category, but I like the idea of starting out small because it gets the attention of Amazon while leaving room for more bang on subsequent days.

In order to be accepted for a Buck Books promotion, you'll need at least 5 reviews and will need to lower your book price to .99 cents. The promotion costs $29.

By the end of the first day, I hit number 3 in the smallest category and number 7 in the largest, with an Amazon ranking of 6,655. I sold 37 books that day due to the promotion. Keep in mind that this book has been promoted on Buck Books twice before, which is why it didn't sell more copies. If you've never run a promotion for your book with them, you can expect to sell more copies. (The first time I ran this book, it sold 60 copies.)

Let your book ride, keeping it at .99 cents the second day because it will be high enough in the rankings to be seen, so you will continue to sell copies throughout that day, too.

My numbers weren't bad at the end of the second day, but I needed to sell a lot more books to get to the number one spot.

Day Three and Four

The next day, I left my book priced at .99 cents and had a Robin Reads promo spot. I was excited about it, because not only are these spots difficult to land (You need a good number of reviews and a professional looking cover to get one), but they tend to push a lot of books. I sold 170 books the day of the promotion and those sales pushed me to bestseller status in two of my three categories.

Here's what my book page looked like at the end of the day:

Product details

File Size: 1750 KB
Print Length: 178 pages
Simultaneous Device Usage: Unlimited
Publisher: Rainmaker Press (March 30, 2016)
Publication Date: March 30, 2016
Sold by: Amazon Digital Services LLC
Language: English
ASIN: B01CTMI7R4
Text-to-Speech: Enabled
X-Ray: Not Enabled
Word Wise: Enabled
Lending: Enabled
Screen Reader: Supported
Enhanced Typesetting: Enabled
Amazon Best Sellers Rank: #1,323 Paid in Kindle Store (See Top 100 Paid in Kindle Store)
  #1 in Kindle Store > Kindle eBooks > Business & Money > Job Hunting & Careers > **Job Hunting**
  #1 in Kindle Store > Kindle eBooks > Business & Money > Entrepreneurship & Small Business > **Starting a Business**
  #2 in Kindle Store > Kindle eBooks > Business & Money > Entrepreneurship & Small Business > **Home-Based**

The price of a Robin Reads promotion varies depending on your book's category, but the nonfiction category, which is where I ran mine, runs $60. You can see the full listing of prices per category at robinreads.com.

Next time I relaunch a book, I will choose the "Featured" category instead of a niche one. It costs $20 more, but has 194,000 subscribers, compared to the 78,000 who subscribe to receive nonfiction book promotions.

On the fourth day, keep your book priced at .99 cents and allow organic sales to come in, which will teach the Amazon algorithm that your book can sell copies over the long haul.

At the end of the fourth day, I had reached bestseller status in 2 of my 3 categories. In fact, I was only a couple hundred points away from the orange tag in the third category, and that's where my sob story comes in.

I told you that we were evacuated from Hurricane Harvey, but what I didn't tell you is that I was in the middle of setting up my promos when the call to evacuate came. I had just about completed my submission to ENT for the final day's promo, which would have easily catapulted me to the top 500 in Amazon's overall ranking and the number 1 spot in all 3 categories. But the hurricane came and I had to leave, and unfortunately we ended up at a ranch in the middle of nowhere with no internet service. In other words, I had no way to manage my relaunch aside from what I'd already done, so I had to let it ride with the 2 promotions I told you about above.

But you can see, I was only a couple of hundred points away from bestseller status in all 3 categories and ENT promotions have netted me hundreds of sales in the past, so it would have been a sure thing.

But alas, the hurricane interfered.

So as you're planning *your* book relaunch, here are the steps you should take for your fifth and sixth day.

Day Five and Six

Ereader News Today (ENT) is a quality book promotion site that will give you great results. The site requires that you have some good reviews, a professional cover, a minimum of 125 pages (except for cookbooks, some nonfiction, and children's books) and a discounted price.

Set your price at .99 cents again for this promotion, and be sure to give yourself enough leeway for scheduling as it can be difficult to land a promotion spot on this site. The site claims a 7 day response time, but in my experience, it oftentimes takes longer than that. You'll pay $50 for a nonfiction book promo spot and varying prices for other categories. You can find a complete price list at ereadernewstoday.com.

The day after your ENT promotion, keep your price set at .99 cents. After these 3 promotions, and with this schedule, you should be at the number 1 spot in all of your categories.

Day 7 and Beyond

Now that you're on the bestseller lists in all your categories, you need to keep selling books to remain high in the listings. Remember, the longer you can stay at the top, the more attention Amazon will pay to your book. The algorithm works like this: your ranking is a direct result of how many books you sold the day before. Essentially, each day's ranking is based on half of the prior day's sales. For example, if you sell 40 books on Monday, on Tuesday, you'll receive a ranking based on 20 book sales. If you sell 30 books on Tuesday, Wednesday's ranking will be based on 15 sales. Can you see why it's so important to have a sustained record of book sales rather than one big day and then nothing?

To continue the momentum, I choose to keep my book priced at .99 for a month after the promotion. I did this because I wanted to continue to bring in sales for the book so it would stay high in the rankings, which would increase the sales of my other books. In fact, sales of the other titles in the series almost doubled because of follow through sales. Having the first book in your series at .99 cents increases your exposure, and remember, exposure on Amazon always results in more book sales.

When Your Ranking Begins to Slip

Inevitably, your book's ranking will begin to slip, and when it does, you'll need to take quick action to prevent its further decline in the rankings. In order to take this last step, you'll need to be enrolled in KDP Select. If you haven't yet enrolled, you should know that most authors attribute about 90 percent of their sales to Amazon, which makes the exclusivity well worth it in my opinion. I've tried going wide several times, but the combination of the lower rankings on Amazon and the paltry sales on other sites keep me coming back to KDP Select. In fact, I'm finished experimenting and have decided to stay exclusive to Amazon for the long haul.

About a month after my promotion, my rankings began to slip. Here's what they looked like:

Print Length: 178 pages
Simultaneous Device Usage: Unlimited
Publisher: Rainmaker Press (March 30, 2016)
Publication Date: March 30, 2016
Sold by: Amazon Digital Services LLC
Language: English
ASIN: B01CTMI7R4
Text-to-Speech: Enabled
X-Ray: Not Enabled
Word Wise: Enabled
Lending: Enabled
Screen Reader: Supported
Enhanced Typesetting: Enabled
Amazon Best Sellers Rank: #40,414 Paid in Kindle Store (See Top 100 Paid in Kindle Store)
#21 in Kindle Store > Kindle eBooks > Business & Money > Job Hunting & Careers > Job Hunting
#28 in Kindle Store > Kindle eBooks > Business & Money > Entrepreneurship & Small Business > Home-Based
#33 in Kindle Store > Kindle eBooks > Business & Money > Entrepreneurship & Small Business > Starting a Business

I knew I had to act fast in order to keep the books in my series selling at a higher rate so their rankings wouldn't slip. So I chose my most popular book in my series, *How to Build a Writing Empire in 30 Days or Less*, and set up a Countdown Deal for it. Why didn't I do that for the book I had just relaunched? Because there are some specific rules you must follow in order to be eligible for a Countdown Deal. Here they are in a nutshell:

- The book has to have the same price for the prior 30 days. This makes it impossible to set up a Countdown Deal for a book you've just relaunched with .99 cent promotions.
- The book has to be enrolled in KDP Select.

Because my goal was to keep people coming to my book pages and seeing my series carousal, it didn't matter which of my books I used for the countdown deal. As long as people were seeing my books, my sales continued.

And here's the beautiful thing: you can run a Countdown Deal for every book in your series every 90 days as long as they're enrolled in KDP Select. That means for my 7 book series, I can run 35 days of Countdown Deals every 3 months—all at no cost to me. Can you see why it's so important to have as many books in your series as possible?

So, let's review. After you've relaunched your book, your goal is to keep your series in the spotlight and the way to do that is to continue to sell. And how do we do that? By being seen by the millions of customers on Amazon. And after a relaunch, Countdown Deals are the ideal method to keep your book in the spotlight.

Remember, although there is a page of current Countdown Deals buyers can browse through on Amazon, these deals work best when a book has high enough rankings to be seen. And then it's like a domino effect. And after a relaunch, all the books in your series will have better rankings because of follow through sales, and that's why this method works so well.

Depending on the number of books in your series, schedule a Countdown Deal for each book as often as you can. For example, because I have 7 books in my series, and Countdown Deals last 5 days, I can schedule 35 days of deals for each 90 day period, which works out to a deal about every 2.5 days. And then as soon as your KDP enrolment refreshes, begin scheduling them all over again. Do this as long as your books stay high enough in the rankings to bring in sufficient sales.

Do it Again

There will come a time when you're just not getting enough traction to satisfy your sales goals, and that's when it time to relaunch another book. Choose the second most popular book in your series, and conduct the same exercises on the next book and then follow the relaunch process outlined in this book. If you carefully follow all the steps in this book again, you should have the same results on your second relaunch, which means all the books in your backlist will benefit once again.

And once the second relaunch has run its course, choose another book in your series and do it again. As long as you continue to update your books, you can relaunch them time and time again.

Remember, as long as you've written a good book and have all of the other essentials, such as a good cover and book description in place, your book can stay up in the rankings for a long time. If one of your books doesn't do well in a relaunch, go back to chapter one and use the Improvement Roadmap to determine why.

Don't Forget About New Releases

This relaunch program works great, but it's important to continue to add books to your backlist so your readers will stay engaged with your brand. Your readers want to hear from you, and keeping your backlist fresh should be an important part of your strategy.

But, here's the thing. If you follow this relaunch schedule, you won't have to publish as often. I have always believed that the road to prosperity as an author is to publish often, but I've come to realize that it just makes more sense to promote the books I've already written in addition to publishing new ones less often. And the same will work for you.

An Unexpected Bonus

As a result of all these sustained sales, I received an unexpected benefit. Amazon contacted me about three weeks after my promotion and extended an invitation to include *How to Work from Home and Make Money: 13 Proven Home-Based Businesses You can Start Today* in their Amazon Prime program. This program allows members of Amazon Prime to read books included in a select group for free. The group consists of about 1,000 books selected by Amazon, and the list changes every 90 days. In exchange for participating in the program, authors are given a one-time bonus between $500 and $1,000—and lots and lots of exposure. After all, the latest estimate shows that there are around 80 million Amazon Prime members.

During the 90 days, authors still receive proceeds from regular book sales and KDP pages read but aren't privy to how many Amazon Prime members read their books for free. But all that exposure will likely result in many more books sold from their backlist.

Now I can't guarantee that everyone who relaunches their book will receive an invitation from Amazon Prime (the program is by invitation only), but my book has been available on Amazon for almost two years and the invitation came only after its relaunch.

Coincidence? I think not.

Chapter Seven: Don't Relaunch Your Book Until You Read This!

Now that you've come to the end of this book, you're likely dying to begin the process of relaunching your book to success. But I want to take a minute to talk to about the necessity of following the plan I've outlined. It's tempting, I know, to relaunch your book right now by skipping a lot of the steps I've outlined and scheduling the promotions right now.

But that won't work, and here's why.

Most of the promotion sites won't schedule a book that doesn't have a professional cover, has a lot of grammatical errors, or doesn't have sufficient reviews. And if you relaunch your book now without a good backlist, you'll only see minimal success. To illustrate this, let's talk about money.

It cost me about $90 to relaunch my book, and after about a month of having it at .99 cents, I had earned less than $200 on the book. If that were my only book, the effort would hardly have been worth it. But because I have 6 other books in my backlist, the payoff was much greater. (And the added bonus from the Amazon Prime program only sweetened the pot.)

In short, you won't see success unless you've completed all of the steps I've outlined in my plan. Let's take a moment to review them.

- **Create an Improvement Roadmap for your book.** This is the most time-consuming step of the process, but one of the most important. You'll need to carefully rethink how your book fits into its genre, take a second look at your cover, rewrite your book description, and reedit your book to ensure it's the best it can be.
- **Use the Lift-Off Strategy by selecting new categories.** The categories your book is in will play a key role in the success or failure of your book's relaunch. Take the time to really study the possibilities and choose an easy one and a difficult one. Then sit back and watch the magic during your relaunch.

- **Make sure you have enough reviews.** Not only will you have trouble getting promo spots on the better promotional sites, but readers won't be as likely to buy your book unless you have a good number of reviews. Strive for 10 at a minimum.
- **Ensure that your internal marketing strategy is in place before you relaunch.** It would be a shame to go to all of this trouble without receiving the benefits of internal marketing. Make sure that you've made it simple for your readers to buy your other books, otherwise you won't reap as many sales.
- **Build your mailing list.** Use the promotion to build your mailing list so your future book launches will see better success rates.
- **Schedule your promotions carefully.** By using the promotion sites I've recommended, you'll get the most for your money and get the attention of Amazon. Your book will be noticed by Amazon's algorithm as an up-and-comer, and that will lead to higher rankings, and even possibly an Amazon Prime invitation.
- **Schedule Countdown Deals.** Continue promoting the books in your series via Countdown Deals as often as you can. This will keep your books up in the rankings so they're seen by more people. This will lead to even more sales.
- **Relaunch 2.0.** Once your ratings begin to drop again, select another book in your series and relaunch it. Be sure to follow the steps outlined in this book for your second relaunch. Continually relaunch your books each time your series begins to drop in the rankings.
- **Publish New Titles.** And don't forget to provide your readers with new titles every few months so they stay interested in your author brand. Be sure to add any new titles you release to your series.

Okay, my friends, if you've completed all of the above steps, you are ready to relaunch your book. A book relaunch can be almost as exciting as the initial launch but it's a different process and must be treated as such. Just follow the steps I've outlined in this book and soon your comatose book will come back to life.

As you're planning your relaunch, feel free to reach out to me at samkernsbooks@gmail.com with any questions, or better yet, your success story!

Now, get out there and pursue your dreams!

Sam

How to Work From Home and Make Money in 2017: 13 Proven Home-Based Businesses You Can Start Today (Work from Home Series: Book 1)

Life is Too Short to Work for Someone Else!

Are you tired of struggling just to get by with a paycheck that doesn't quite stretch far enough? Or are you one of the millions of people who are out of work in an economy gone bad? Maybe you long to be your own boss so you can set your own schedule and choose the path your life will take.

Whatever it is that brought you to this page, you're obviously looking for answers. **The good news is you've come to the right place.**

I've spent the past 20 years working for myself, and I would never dream of punching another clock or trudging to someone else's office every day to collect a meager paycheck. That's because I've discovered the secret: when you work for yourself, you're happier, more productive, and you have unlimited earning potential.

After all, **why would you want to work so hard to fund someone else's dreams?**

Working for myself has allowed me to live a lifestyle that many people can only dream about. I have the flexibility to create the life I want, take days off when I need to, and I decide how much money I make by choosing the hours I work.

But don't be fooled. Working from home at a home-based business isn't easy. It takes hard work and dedication to build a successful business that will make money.

In my book, I'm pleased to offer you **10 proven, realistic ways to work from home and earn a great income.** And I won't just offer you a brief explanation of each method like some other books do.

In each chapter, I provide you with the information and facts you need to determine if that business is right for you. But I don't stop there. I'll also give you important links and resources, so if you decide you want to pursue one of the home-based business ideas listed in this book, **you'll have everything you need to begin.**

So, the choice is yours. Will you wake up tomorrow morning and spend your day funding someone else's dream, or will you finally take the steps needed to claim your own success?

Why not start right now by buying How to Work From Home and Make Money? It's one of the most important things you'll do to begin the process of achieving your own dreams.

Click here to go to Amazon and buy the book!

How to Build a Writing Empire in 30 Days or Less (Work from Home Series: Book 2)

Do You Want to Make a Real Living as a Writer? You'll Have to Throw Out Everything You Know

Let me guess—you're a talented writer who is willing to do whatever it takes to make a full-time living by writing. You've read countless articles and books on the subject, followed the suggestions in them, but you just can't seem to make the income leap.

Or you may be a new writer who is convinced that you're missing something because your own experience isn't matching up to what you've read is possible.

Or perhaps you've been moonlighting as a freelance writer for years, and you're convinced that it's simply not possible to quit your "real" job and do what you love full time.

Let me tell you a secret. You've been lied to. Yes, you heard me correctly. **Lied. To.**

The truth is, only about 10 percent of writers earn enough working full time to support themselves. *Ten percent.* That's not something all those other how-to writing books spend a lot of time on, is it?

Luckily, there's a real solution.

I know this because I've been doing it myself for years. But in order to be successful in this business, you'll have to turn the current freelance writing working model on its head. In fact, you pretty much **have to throw everything you thought you knew out the window.**

What I'm talking about is a new system. One that doesn't limit a freelance writer's ability to make a great income because of time constraints. I'm talking about earning a living anyone would be proud of.

In this book, I'll show you how to create your own Writing Empire in 30 days or less. You'll learn:

- Why most freelancers can't make a decent living—and what to do about it
- How to structure your writing business in a way that works best for your lifestyle
- How to brand your business to attract the type of clients you want
- Where to find clients and how to land the jobs
- How to structure your time in order to earn the highest possible income in the shortest amount of time
- How to hire a team of qualified, motivated writers who will help you build your Empire

And that's not all. I'll give you a **step-by-step plan** that will lead you to success. This plan looks **in detail** at your first:

- Day
- Week
- Month
- And beyond

Like I said, I structured my own business this way, so let my experience help you achieve your dreams.

Are you ready to get serious about your writing career and make some serious money? Start right now by downloading the book and learn how to make a real living with writing!

Click here to buy the book on Amazon!

How to Start a Home-Based Food Business: Turn Your Foodie Love into Serious Cash with a Food Business Startup (Work from Home Series Book 3)

Finally, a Comprehensive Guide to Starting a Food Business!

Do your insides jump for joy when you see a perfectly frosted cupcake or cookie? Or do you love the look of violet lavender syrup or a mouthwatering strawberry and lime jam? Or are you more of a savory person and melt when you see a jar of homemade salsa or seasoned nuts with just the right amount of spices?

If food excites you as much as it does me, you just might be a foodie. And in today's food-centered world, there is serious money to be made with your passion.

Food consumption has really changed in the past decade, and now more than ever, people want to know what's in their food, where it came from and who made it. That's bad news for businesses that mass produce food, but great news for those in the cottage food industry.

You see, in the past individuals who wanted to sell food were required to involve the state health inspectors and lease commercial kitchens in order to sell to the public. Obviously, that prevented a lot of people from pursuing their food dreams. But now many states have passed **cottage food laws** that are designed to give home chefs and bakers the right to produce products from their homes and sell them to the public.

If you've read my other books, you know I'm a serial entrepreneur. I've opened and closed many businesses in my lifetime, and there's nothing I love more than taking an idea and turning it into a smoothly run, profitable business. And this book was born of that desire.

Let me explain.

I bake. There—it's out in the open. I'm a guy and I bake. Can we please move on?

Specifically, I bake specialty brownies that are so good I've had local stores approach me and ask me to sell them wholesale, and I get phone calls from friends begging me to bake a batch. Yeah, my brownies are that good.

So when I heard about the changes in the law allowing people to start home-based food businesses, my entrepreneurial mind starting spinning. I have a great product, so in my mind, there was no reason why I couldn't create a profitable business. I should just open one, right?

Fortunately, that's not the way I roll. I have never simply opened a business and learned as I go—instead I conduct so much research that I know absolutely everything there is to know before I begin. In other words, I leave no room for error. I want the information up front so I can make the best decisions and build a successful business.

Otherwise, what's the point?

So, when the idea of opening a cottage food business occurred to me, I began researching and I didn't stop for months. That's where this book comes in. There is a lot to know about this type of business, and one thing I learned is that there is simply nowhere that you can get all of the information in one place.

Until this book.

Don't believe me? Take a look at all the other books on the subject and just see if the author provides a state-by-state index of all the cottage food laws. Let me save you some time. They don't.

And recipes that fit into the guidelines of the laws? Nope, you won't find them in other books. How about serious insight into how to best brand, package and market your home-based food business? You'll only find that in this book.

So, let my obsessive research into business ideas, along with my entrepreneurial skills, help you in your own business. I've done the hard work for you, so **all you have do is follow the plan I've outlined in this book and you'll be on your way to building your very own food business**. And all the newbie questions you have but are too embarrassed to ask? I had them, too and I've included the answers to them in this book.

If you're ready to pursue your foodie dreams, download the book and learn everything you need to know!

Click here to buy the book on Amazon!

How to Brand Your Home-Based Business: Why Business Branding is Crucial for Even the Smallest Startups (Work from Home Series Book 4)

How to

Your Home-Based
Business

Sam Kerns

What's the Difference Between a Successful Home-Based Business and One that Fails? Branding.

Home-based business startups are exploding all across the world as more and more people realize that the best way to take control of your life—and your finances—is to work for yourself. But what many people forget to do is brand their small business.

That's a mistake. You see, business branding isn't only for the big guys. Home-based business owners also need to focus on creating a brand that will speak to their customers and forge that ever-important bond between the business and the public.

But home-based business owners shouldn't play by the same rules when it comes to branding their business. For starters, most solopreneurs don't have the finances to pay big shot logo designers, graphic artists and copywriters, not to mention the cash to invest in top-notch packaging and marketing efforts.

And why would you want to?

Building a brand doesn't have to be expensive or complicated, but it does require a plan and the knowledge about how to best create the right brand and then use it to build your business.

If you own a home-based business and can't figure out why you're not meeting your goals, could it be that you haven't take the time to properly brand it? And if you're just starting out, you shouldn't even think about opening your doors until you've branded your business for success.

In this book, I'll show you:

- What branding is and why your business can't truly succeed without it
- The biggest benefits you'll reap from a business brand
- The 7 mistakes most people make when building a brand—and how to avoid them
- How to build a brand in today's high-tech world
- A step-by-step guide to brand building that will work for any type of business (along with links and resources)

Don't let your hard work go to waste. Increase your market share (and profits) in your current home-based business, or start your new business on the right foot by reading this important book.

Click Here to Buy The Book from Amazon!

How to Publish a Book on Amazon: Real Advice from Someone Who's Doing It Well (Work from Home Series: Book 5)

Are you tired of "how to publish books" that are full of fluff and no real information? So was I.

Before I began my publishing career with Kindle books, I read just about everything out there, looking for real answers to questions I had about the industry. But much to my disappointment, most of the books were filled with fluff or stories of people who "hit it big" without really telling me how or why.

I determined to jump in and learn for myself—and that's exactly what I did. I started with my first book, How to Work from Home and Make Money, and then quickly published three more. I was looking for the topic of my fifth book when it hit me—**why not share what I've learned with the people who still haven't made the leap and published their own book?**

It all began when I received an email from a book promotion site. One of the features was a how to book about publishing Kindle books, so out of curiosity, I followed the link and read the reviews. And sure enough, the page was full of people complaining that the book didn't contain any valuable information.

So here's what I decided to do. Write a book that answers all of the real questions without painting an unrealistic view of the possibilities. I answer things like:

- How to pick book topics that will sell. (Why it's important, and what I've done right—and wrong.)
- How to write a book in 30 days or less. (And take weekends off)
- How to conduct research for your book.
- How to make your own covers for free.
- The pros and cons of pre-releasing your book.
- When you should enroll your book in Kindle Unlimited (And when you shouldn't.)

- How to format your book yourself. (Including the clickable table of contents) And how to get it done for cheap if you don't want to.
- Why you need a paperback version. (And how to create one)
- Why you may need an audio book (And how to get one for free)
- How to get your book translated into other languages for free (And why you should)
- Why ranking matters (And what to do if your book isn't ranking well.)
- How to market your book. (Including links and contact information for the people I use)
- What to do after you publish your first book.
- How much you can REALLY expect to make with Kindle publishing

I talk about the mistakes I've made so you don't make them, too. And I provide you with **step-by-step instructions and relevant links for all of the above areas**—and more. In other words, this book is the ONLY book you'll need to start a career publishing Kindle books.

If you've been dreaming of publishing a book, but don't know where to start—or if you've already published but can't find success—this may be the book you've been waiting for.

Why not take the first step toward your publishing career and download it right now? I promise you won't find any fluff or useless information in it. Just an actionable guide that answers the questions no one else will.

Click here to buy the book from Amazon!

The Writer's Toolkit Boxed Set (Work from Home: Books 2 and 5)

Two bestselling books in one boxed set!

Click here to buy the boxed set from Amazon!

The Weekend Writer: How to Write a Non-Fiction Book in Two Months even if You Have a Full-Time Job (Work from Home Series: Book 6)

Do you fear you'll never publish a book because you don't have time to write?

Let me guess—you're a writer, but so far, the book you *know* will be a big hit is stuck inside your head because you simply don't have the time to sit down and write it. You've probably been told that you need to block out mass chunks of time to write a book, but I'm here to tell you that's just not true.

It's possible to write a quality book in two months—writing only on the weekends—using my step-by-step plan.

I'm not talking about putting out some of the junk that passes for books these days. I'm talking about writing a full-length book you'll be proud to put your name on, and readers will be thrilled they bought.

Here's what you'll find in this revolutionary book:

- How to get in the right mindset to write on a limited schedule
- How to choose your book topic so it sells
- How to outline your book in a way that makes writing it easier
- How to set up a no-fail writing schedule so you can meet your deadline
- How to use productivity hacks that will help you stay on track and accomplish your goal
- How to edit as you go
- A weekend-by-weekend guide that shows you the exact steps you need to take to have a finished book in just two months—only writing on the weekends.

Bonus! Free Chapter Preview: How to Build a Writing Empire in 30 Days or Less

Chapter 1: Why Being a Good Writer Just Isn't Enough Any More

The Big Lie

Let me guess—you're a talented writer who is willing to do whatever it takes to make a full-time living by writing. You've read countless articles and books on the subject, followed the suggestions in them, but you just can't seem to make the income leap. Or you may be a new writer who is convinced that you're missing something because your own experience just isn't matching up to what others say is possible. Or perhaps you've been moonlighting as a freelance writer for years, and you're convinced that it's simply not possible to quit your "real" job and do what you love full-time.

Let me tell you a secret. You've been lied to. Yes, you heard me correctly. **Lied. To.**

Our culture teaches us that if we work hard enough and have at least some talent, we can become a success and accomplish our dreams. I'm not necessarily disagreeing with that. In fact, I wholeheartedly believe in the American Dream. But what I am saying is that the freelance writing business isn't like most other career choices, and the uniqueness of the profession requires you to think a little outside of the box if you want to make a real living from it.

Take me as an example. I've considered myself a writer my entire life. When I was 10 years old, I knew that writing was the career—the only career—that I wanted. I took the first step when I reached my early twenties—after suffering miserably in an office environment for a few years—and sent queries to magazines and book publishers. (This was before it was possible to act as your own indie publisher.) I was lucky because unlike many of my peers, I didn't seem to have any trouble landing assignments, and I was even given a book contract with a publisher in my second year.

But there was a problem. Despite my early success, I was nowhere near making what I needed to in order to earn a full-time living. I began to wonder what was wrong. I was working 50 to 60 hours a week, and even if I'd been able to secure more writing assignments, I wouldn't have had time to complete them. So instead of pursuing my writing dreams, I began to open other businesses, and while I achieved success with them, I couldn't let go of my desire to work as a writer. There had to be a way, the entrepreneur side of me said, but for the life of me, I couldn't figure it out.

Something certainly wasn't adding up.

The One Percent

Determined that it must be something I was doing wrong, I set out to find the solution. I read every book I could find about how to make a living as a freelance writer, but was dismayed to learn that I was already doing everything the books recommended. The "experts" on the subject suggested that I if I would only follow their time-proven plan, I'd be able to quit my day job in time and pursue my dream.

But that simply wasn't true. I was working hard and following all the expert advice, and I still wasn't earning an income large enough to support myself.

And then I came across a startling statistic that changed the course of my writing career and eventually led to this book. Are you sitting down?

Only about 10 percent of writers earn enough from working full-time to support themselves. *Ten percent.*

And the figures haven't improved over time. According to the Author's Guild, about half of the full-time writers they surveyed earn less than $12,000 a year in income, which falls below the federal poverty level. Not exactly what you had in mind when thinking about pursuing a writing career, is it?

And it's not much better in the U.K. According to a study commissioned by the Author's Licensing and Collecting Society, only 11.5 percent of freelancers who dedicate almost all of their time to writing earn enough money to support themselves.

Are you kidding me? What happened to doing our best and becoming a success? How about the fact that most writers end up working ridiculous hours just to keep up with the demand? What about that *American Dream*?

After I recovered from the shock, I became determined to uncover the secret of the ten percent. What made them so special? Were they that much above the cut in their skills? Did they have inside connections, or were they just plain lucky?

Here's what I found. A percentage of that ten percent are bestselling novelists, nonfiction writers who are experts in their field, or advertising and marketing copywriters who spent years building their reputation as the go-to person in sales copy.

The smallest portion of the ten percent are those writers who have managed to get in with the highest paying markets (sometimes thousands of dollars per article) and receive a steady flow of assignments from them. This generally takes years to accomplish.

But hey, what about the rest of the writers? Those who mostly work in the midrange markets and the internet? (In other words, the other 90 percent). Shouldn't they be able to make a decent living doing what they love, too?

That's when I discovered that it's all in the math.

It Just Doesn't Add Up

I decided to calculate how many hours I would have to write each month in order to earn a living that would afford me and my family a comfortable living. So I set a target income and worked backwards from there. My bottom line base figure was $100,000 per year. Yours might be different, and I encourage you to give this part of the process some serious thought.

First, add up your monthly obligations such as mortgage or rent, utilities, car payments, food, and the rest your living expenses. Don't forget to account for property taxes, insurance, college educations, and income taxes.

Next, you should add in the amount of money you want for savings, entertainment, and the amount of disposable income you'd be content with. Remember, we're not just talking about "making it." I want you to write down a figure that will comfortably sustain you and your family while putting money away for your retirement. As artists, we have to get a new mindset. The old thinking says that if you're lucky enough to do something you love, you will probably suffer financially. That's yesterday's thought process. I'm telling you, it is possible to do what you love AND make a good living.

Like I said, my target goal was $100,000, but yours should be individualized for your lifestyle. Now, take that number and divide it by 12, 52, and 260 (the average number of workdays in a year) to give you a rough idea of what you need to earn monthly, weekly, and daily. My $100,000 figure looks something like this:

Yearly Goal = $100,000

Monthly Goal = $8,333

Weekly Goal = $1,923

Daily Goal = $385

Next, I figured the average price customers pay per article. Now, this can be tricky because the rates are so diverse, depending on the level of experience of the writer and the type of article being assigned. For the purposes of this exercise, let's concentrate on internet content articles, as that's what most people will start out with in this business.

Typically, new writers start out at about $25 per article for internet content, and once they build a good portfolio, they can demand much higher rates. So, for this book, I'm going to assume that many of you are just starting out and use that rate. Please feel free to substitute your higher rate if you've already surpassed this level.

So, using the target goal of $100,000 and a $25 per article payout, here's what it looks like:

In order to earn $100,000 per year, you would have to produce 4,000 articles a year. That means you would have to write 333 article a month, or 83 a week. And if broken down into the 260 workdays in a year, that means in order to earn the target income, it would be necessary to write just over 15 articles a day.

Are you still with me? I know, it's discouraging and at this point, you might feel like it's not even possible. But good news is coming. Stay with me, okay?

Now that you understand how many articles it will take to get to your desired income, let's talk about how many hours you'll have to spend to write them.

Again, this will differ depending on your experience. A seasoned writer can complete an internet content article in a little under an hour, but a newbie may take two hours. Let's average that for our purposes, and use an hour and a half. Here's the amount of hours you would need to spend to meet the $100,000 per year goal.

- You would need to work 6,000 hours a year in order to write 4,000 articles a year.

- You would need to work 499.5 hours a month in order to write 333 articles a month.

- You would need to work 124.5 hours a week in order to write 83 articles a week.

- You would need to work 22.5 hours a day in order to write 15 articles a day.

Hang on, it's going to get worse before it gets better. (But remember, I have a solution.)

The Other Part of Writing

Let me break this to you gently: when working as a freelance writer, writing is only a portion of the tasks you'll need to complete every day in order to run a profitable business. And your other responsibilities? You guessed it. They're time consuming. Let's take a look at the other things you'll have to do in order to maintain your business.

Marketing

You will receive no assignments unless you sell yourself. We will go deeply into the how's and whys of marketing your writing Empire, but for now you should know that you will need to spend approximately two hours a day querying editors, bidding on jobs, looking for new clients, and managing your portfolio. So, you can automatically add two hours per day to all of the above figures.

Accounts Payable and Client Communications

Two other areas you will spend a great amount of time on are client communications and ensuring that you're paid for the jobs you've completed. Your clients will want to communicate with you before you begin work on an assignment in order to make sure you understand the scope of the project. Many of them will also want you to check in during the project so you can ask any questions you may have or update them on the status of the project. And once the project is completed, the client will either approve the work or ask you for modifications. Some clients are fine communicating via email, while others expect you to be available on Skype or even the phone.

Effective communication with clients is critical in order to establish long lasting business relationships. In other words, it will not only help you gain new clients, but it will also help you retain your hard earned accounts.

And once you've completed a project, you'll need to invoice the client, and then stay on top of that invoice until it's paid. All clients are different in how they want you to invoice them. Many use PayPal, while others prefer to put a check in the mail. Some will ask you to create a professional invoice, while others will simply ask you to email them an invoice. If the buyer hired you via your website, they will have paid your fee before you started the project. And if you work with clients on bid sites, each site has its own invoicing requirements that you'll need to learn.

So, how much time does all this take? Again, it depends on how many ongoing jobs you have and how many clients you work with, but it's safe to say that you should plan on about an hour and a half per day on these tasks.

Wait a minute. If we add three and a half hours to your workday for marketing, invoicing, and client communications, that means you'd have to work 26 hours a day to earn the target goal of $100,000 per year. That may be a problem, because the last time I checked, there were only 24 hours in a day.

That's not something all those other how-to writing books spend a lot of time on, is it? But now that I've uncovered the problem, we can talk about the solution. And there *is* a solution.

Thinking like a Twenty-First Century Writer

At this point, you must realize that there are simply not enough hours in the day to do all it takes to earn a real living as a full-time freelance writer. Time is the enemy. It's the number one reason so many writers spend years struggling on an "artist's" income (Sorry, but there's nothing romantic about that when you're trying to support a family), or end up taking a "day job" in order to help ends meet. If you're already a freelancer, how many times have you wished you could clone yourself several times over to be able to produce more content so you could earn a decent living?

Exactly.

What if I told you that you could double, triple, or even quadruple your time, allowing you to not only increase your income, but also spend more time pursuing the types of writing projects *you* want to?

What I'm talking about is building a writing Empire—an organization of writers that all work for you under your direction. I'm talking about taking your passion, your skill, and making big business out of it. I'm talking about transforming the way you get business and the way you produce it.

I'm taking about finally bringing the freelance writing industry into the twenty-first century.

This is not just an idea—it's something I've done myself for years, and it transformed my professional life in a matter of months.

It can transform your world, too.

Read on and let me show you a step-by-step plan you can use to build your own writing Empire.

After all, why should the big boys have all the fun?

Want to keep reading? <u>Download the bestselling book</u> and start pursuing your dreams!

Read my books for FREE by signing up for my mailing list! Click here or go to RainMakerPress.com